DATE DUE

80			
OCT 1 0			
1/14/97 WHM R			
FEB 2 4 1997			

Demco, Inc. 38-293

SPORTS GREAT ANFERNEE HARDAWAY

—Sports Great Books —

Sports Great Jim Abbott
(ISBN 0-89490-395-0)

Sports Great Troy Aikman
(ISBN 0-89490-593-7)

Sports Great Charles Barkley
(ISBN 0-89490-386-1)

Sports Great Larry Bird
(ISBN 0-89490-368-3)

Sports Great Barry Bonds
(ISBN 0-89490-595-3)

Sports Great Bobby Bonilla
(ISBN 0-89490-417-5)

Sports Great Roger Clemens
(ISBN 0-89490-284-9)

Sports Great John Elway
(ISBN 0-894909-282-2)

Sports Great Patrick Ewing
(ISBN 0-89490-369-1)

Sports Great Steffi Graf
(ISBN 0-89490-597-X)

Sports Great Anfernee Hardaway
(ISBN 0-89490-758-1)

Sports Great Orel Hershiser
(ISBN 0-89490-389-6)

Sports Great Bo Jackson
(ISBN 0-89490-281-4)

Sports Great Magic Johnson
(Revised and Expanded)
(ISBN 0-89490-348-9)

Sports Great Michael Jordan
(ISBN 0-89490-370-5)

Sports Great Mario Lemieux
(ISBN 0-89490-596-1)

Sports Great Karl Malone
(ISBN 0-89490-599-6)

Sports Great Joe Montana
(ISBN 0-89490-371-3)

Sports Great Hakeem Olajuwon
(ISBN 0-89490-372-1)

Sports Great Shaquille O'Neal
(ISBN 0-89490-594-5)

Sports Great Kirby Puckett
(ISBN 0-89490-392-6)

Sports Great Jerry Rice
(ISBN 0-89490-419-1)

Sports Great Cal Ripkin, Jr.
(ISBN 0-89490-387-X)

Sports Great David Robinson
(ISBN 0-89490-373-X)

Sports Great Nolan Ryan
(ISBN 0-89490-394-2)

Sports Great Barry Sanders
(ISBN 0-89490-418-3)

Sports Great John Stockton
(ISBN 0-89490-598-8)

Sports Great Darryl Strawberry
(ISBN 0-89490-291-1)

Sports Great Isiah Thomas
(ISBN 0-89490-374-8)

Sports Great Hershel Walker
(ISBN 0-89490-207-5)

SPORTS GREAT ANFERNEE HARDAWAY

George Rekela

—Sports Great Books —

ENSLOW PUBLISHERS, INC.
44 Fadem Road   P.O. Box 38
Box 699   Aldershot
Springfield, N.J. 07081   Hants GU12 6BP
U.S.A.   U.K.

Library of Congress Cataloging-in-Publication Data

Rekela, George, 1943–
Sports great Anfernee Hardaway/ George Rekela.
    p. cm.—(Sports great books)
Includes index.
ISBN 0-89490-758-1
    1. Hardaway, Anfernee—Juvenile Literature. 2. Basketball
players—United States—Biography—Juvenile Literature. I. Title.
II. Series.
GV884.H24R45   1995
796.323'092 B–dc20

                                                95-20298
                                                   CIP
                                                   AC

Printed in the United States of America

10 9 8 7 6 5 4 3 2 1

Illustration Credits: © Copyright Brian Drake, pp. 9, 45, 53; George Rekela, p. 60;
Naismith Memorial Hall of Fame photo, p. 24; Photo obtained with permission
from University of Memphis archives, pp. 13, 22, 29, 30, 41; Photo by Steve Jones
from University of Memphis Archives, pp. 16, 37; REUTERS/BETTMAN, pp. 8,
50, 55; *Sports Illustrated* photo, p. 17; STAR TRIBUNE/Minneapolis-St. Paul,
Photo by Marlin Levinson, p. 36.

Cover Photo © Copyright Brian Drake

Contents

Chapter 1

The National Basketball Association has seen its share of exciting games in its nearly fifty years of existence, but few could compare with the nationally televised contest between the Orlando Magic and the Chicago Bulls on February 26, 1995, at the Orlando Arena before a sellout crowd of 16,010 spectators.

Orlando entered the game with a 41–13 win-loss record, best in the NBA, but this didn't faze the proud Bulls, three-time world champions from 1991 through 1993. The Bulls had an advantage in that Orlando's all-pro center and leading scorer, Shaquille O'Neal, would be sitting out the game while on suspension from the league. And, the Magic's star power forward, Horace Grant, an ex-Bull, would miss the game because of painful back spasms.

The scene was set for a Chicago victory. The Bulls could taste it, but they failed to reckon with Orlando's slender point guard, Anfernee "Penny" Hardaway.

Hardaway had always played in O'Neal's massive shadow during his two years of NBA competition. In all the league

7

With Anfernee Hardaway and Shaquille O'Neal blocking Chicago Bulls center Luc Longley, the Magic beat the Bulls in 1994.

cities, the crowds came to see Shaq play. That Hardaway, himself an all-pro, was Shaq's teammate was frequently remembered only as an afterthought. Certainly, television executives wanted to showcase O'Neal whenever they could. Now, with Shaq on the bench, the cameras would have to be switched to focus on Hardaway.

All his life, Hardaway had faced pressure situations. Each time, he had triumphed. In the locker room before the game, he told his teammates that he realized what the situation was, that the national television spotlight would be on him. He vowed to put on the performance of his life. He did not fail.

The Bulls played well; they led by 8 points with only 6 minutes left in the game. Hardaway had played nearly the entire game for the Magic, scoring on a dazzling variety of jump shots, offensive rebounds, and three-point goals. When he wasn't scoring himself, he was passing the ball to his teammates, who often worked their way free for baskets. In short, he was playing the game of a lifetime, but he still couldn't push his team into the lead.

Less than 2 minutes remained, and Chicago led by 5

Against the Chicago Bulls, Hardaway played the game of a lifetime.

points. Dennis Scott of the Magic scored on a long three-point basket, and Orlando drew within two. Then, with 27 seconds showing on the clock, Scott had the ball and drove toward the Bulls' Pete Myers who fouled him. Scott calmly sank both free throws. The game was tied at 103–103.

Chicago elected to go for a three-point shot to win the game. The ball was passed back and forth among them behind the three-point line; then all-star forward Scottie Pippen called for a time out with 7 seconds left. Both teams regrouped.

What happened next was one of those magical moments that most basketball fans wait a lifetime to see. The Bulls' Toni Kukoc got the ball and wheeled toward the free throw line. Suddenly, he appeared to have the ball stripped away from him by Orlando's Nick Anderson.

"He tried to spin," Anderson said later, "and I just tipped the ball from behind."

Time seemed to slow. In fact, to Hardaway, it appeared that everything was happening like a slow-motion ballet. He later recalled scooping up the loose ball. The basket was 60 feet away. He glanced at the clock; only 3.9 seconds remained. Was there enough time?

Dribbling the ball before him, he took off, making long, graceful strides. Just past the free throw line, he left the ground, attaining the power of flight was he approached the basket. He slammed the ball through the hoop, and the capacity crowd went wild. He looked up at the clock. He had made the winning basket with 0.7 seconds to spare.

Veteran fans in the audience shook their heads. No game had ever ended on such a spectacular note.

"I wasn't worried," a serene Hardaway told teammates and sportswriters. "I knew I had enough time."

Chapter 2

Anfernee Deon Hardaway was born in Memphis, Tennessee, on July 18, 1971, to Fae Hardaway and Ed Golden. "When he was born," said his mother, "his hands were so big it looked like he was wearing gloves." Fae Hardaway was nineteen years old when her son was born. "Fae was just a child herself," recalled her mother, Louise, Anfernee's grandmother. "Fae was young and running wild," Louise said. The responsibility for raising Anfernee would fall into his grandmother's hands.

Louise Hardaway, her husband Sylvester, her sons Lester and John, and her daughter Gloria, had arrived in Memphis on New Year's Day, 1950. They were a family of poor Arkansas sharecroppers who finally had raised enough money— $365—to purchase a clapboard house at 2977 Forest Avenue. These economical houses in their neighborhood were made of wooden boards thin on one edge and thicker on the other, to allow overlapping.

Two years later, a second daughter, Fae, was born. Louise Hardaway had found work as a cook and maid, and later was employed by the Memphis public school system as a cafeteria cook. Louise and Sylvester Hardaway separated in 1956, and he died nineteen years later.

Anfernee Hardaway was named for a classmate of his mother's at nearby Lester High School. "I thought Anfernee was such a beautiful name," Fae Hardaway said. As he grew older, Anfernee was seldom called that. His grandmother, in her joy upon seeing him in the maternity hospital, had nicknamed him "Pretty." No one is sure how, as the years passed, "Pretty" became "Penny." Most agree, though, that neighbors called the boy Penny because they routinely misunderstood his grandmother.

Louise Hardaway and her grandson were familiar neighborhood fixtures, walking hand in hand to the Early Grove Baptist Church for regular services.

Anfernee recalled that "she always had me home indoors before the sun went down." When the streetlights went on in Memphis, it was the boy's signal to be at home, safe inside the house, alone with his grandmother.

Young Anfernee remembered standing in the doorway watching friends hang out in the street well after dark. "There I was, wanting to cry because I didn't think it was fair. I thought, 'Man, I can't wait to get out of here.' My grade school teacher once told me, 'You're going to thank your grandmother one day.' And I do now."

Louise Hardaway might have been too careful, but she believed she had good reason. Alcohol and drugs were always around on the streets of Memphis, a rough river town. "It seemed to me," she said, "that some boys raised on Forest Avenue wound up in jail or the workhouse for robbing and stealing. One wound up getting life in prison. For a long time, I didn't let that boy out of my sight."

Boyhood friend and Memphis State teammate Elliott Perry

Penny Hardaway's boyhood friend in Memphis, Elliot Perry (left), later recalled that Hardaway leaned solely on his grandmother for guidance.

recalled that Hardaway leaned solely on his grandmother. "She did so much for Anfernee. She raised him right."

After his grade school years, though, it became more difficult for Louise to watch her grandson's every move. He would sneak over to Lester Community Center's asphalt playgrounds where there were hoops and backboards mounted on steel poles. Eventually, with Louise's permission, the boy was spending eight to nine hours a day at Lester playing outdoor basketball. "It got to where other boys came, played, went home, ate, came back, and I'd still be there playing. Mostly I played by myself." It just felt right for him to be there. It was where he belonged.

Anfernee became a quiet loner. Basketball gave him the chance to enjoy himself without having to rely on the company of others. All he needed was a ball and a hoop. He could work at the game all alone, perfecting his dribbling, shooting, passing, and rebounding skills at his own pace.

As the years passed, Anfernee grew faster and taller than his classmates. He was willing to walk more than two miles to attend Treadwell High School, known nationally for its outstanding basketball program.

Unfortunately, at Treadwell he paid little attention to academics. Counselors were more interested in Anfernee's athletic ability. As a skinny freshman, he averaged 10 points a game for one of the best high school basketball teams in the United States.

By the time he was a sophomore, Hardaway had raised his average by 17 points a game. during his junior year, he averaged 32 points, 8 rebounds, 7 assists, 3 steals, and 2 blocked shots for a team that won an astounding 38 games and lost only 3. In the words of talent scout Sonny Vaccaro, "When Penny Hardaway goes to the basket, very few people can stop him."

Anfernee's senior season at Treadwell was one that most high school hoopsters can only dream about. He led the state of Tennessee with a scoring average of 36.3 points per game, including a 58-point outburst in a game with Mitchell High School. He averaged 10 rebounds, 6 assists, 3 steals, and 3 blocked shots a game. Moreover, he shot 56 percent from the field and averaged 3 three-point baskets per game.

Honors fell like rain upon Hardaway. He was named a first-team high school All-American by *Basketball Times*. *Parade* magazine selected Hardaway as the National High School Player of the Year. He was named Mr. Basketball in Tennessee. He was selected to play in the Olympic Festival basketball tournament in Minneapolis. Anfernee Hardaway was sitting on top of the world.

Hardaway and his grandmother weren't ready for the amount of phone calls and letters suddenly reaching their home. College recruiters from all over the nation were after Hardaway, wanting him to star on the basketball court.

For a while, he considered the University of Arkansas, but Louise Hardaway put a stop to that notion. She wanted her grandson close to home. In the end, he agreed. He would go to Memphis State University.

The prestigious and influential *Street & Smith's Basketball Yearbook* annually lists "college freshmen of influence." The 1990–91 yearbook prominently mentions freshmen Grant Hill, Shawn Bradley, Eric Montross, Khalid Reeves, Damon Bailey, and Rodney Rodgers. Nowhere does the name Anfernee Hardaway appear. Why the apparent snub?

Hardaway was probably the best high school basketball player in the country before he graduated from Memphis's Treadwell High School. He would soon learn, however, that he would have to sit out his freshman year at Memphis State University because he was admitted under the guidelines of the National Collegiate Athletic Association's (NCAA) By-law 5-1(j), a controversial measure better known as Proposition 48.

At Treadwell, the faculty apparently was too amazed by Hardaway's basketball performances to notice that he wasn't keeping up with his schoolwork. It wasn't because he was a slow learner, his grades at Memphis State would soon prove him to be highly intelligent. Hardaway was just too single-minded. Basketball took precedence over everything else, including homework. He paid dearly for it by losing a year of college eligibility.

"When I graduated from high school," Hardaway remembered, "My grade point average was 2.2, and I couldn't pass the ACT (college entrance examination)." Hardaway's grades did not meet the standards considered acceptable in order for him to play basketball. The result was that he had to give up his first year of basketball competition at Memphis State while being branded as "academically ineligible" under Proposition 48.

Nevertheless, the invitation to the Olympic Festival Games was still open. The Olympic Festival games were started by the United States Olympic Committee in 1978 to introduce promising young American athletes to the intensity of Olympic competition. Athletes are selected for Olympic Festival participation by the national governing body of their sport, then divided into four teams representing the North, South, East, and West. Medal awards, elaborate opening and closing ceremonies, and an athletes' village create an Olympic-style atmosphere. Olympic Festivals are held every non-Olympic year. In 1990, when Minneapolis was chosen as the site, some three thousand athletes and "future Olympians" competed for medals in thirty-seven sports, one of which was basketball.

Hardaway packed his bags and headed for Minneapolis. When Penny arrived, all of the attention was focused on

Because of NCAA Proposition 48 regulations, Hardaway could only sit on the sidelines his freshman year at Memphis State University.

Anfernee Hardaway drew the attention of Olympic officials and was chosen to play in the 1990 Olympic Festival in Minneapolis for the South.

Shaquille O'Neal, who had averaged 13.9 points, 12 rebounds, and blocked 12 shots per game as a freshman at Louisiana State. Hardaway was assigned to O'Neal's tournament team, the South, coached by O'Neal's mentor at LSU, Dale Brown.

Coach Brown seemed too involved with his own LSU star to pay much attention to Hardaway. The coach told others that he had heard Hardaway played out-of-control basketball. Also, Hardaway had to deal with the shame of Prop 48. To Coach Brown, the media, and most fans, this meant that he probably was too stupid to be a star player, let alone to carry on meaningful conversation. Wherever he appeared at festival events, Hardaway seemed to be invisible. The spotlight was continually on Shaquille O'Neal and Coach Brown.

Hardaway recalled that if people did speak to him, they seemed to think he was stupid. "They told me I screwed up and should be playing college ball in 1990." Instead, he would sit the year out.

All of this only fueled his drive to succeed. There were four teams in the tournament; North, South, East, and West. Dale Brown's South team played its first game against the team from the West. Hardaway was tense, and his performance reflected it. He hit on only 2 shots (out of 10) from the field. Both, however, were from three-point land. The crowd had come to see Shaq perform, and he didn't disappoint them, scoring 26 points.

The second game pitted the South against the North and its star players, Eric Montross, Damon Bailey, Jimmy Jackson, and J.R. Rider. Brown's team lost 128–121, despite 39 points from O'Neal. Few paid attention to Hardaway, although he shook the first-game jitters to score 21 points.

Next, the South team took on the East and came away 136–125 winners, setting the stage for the Gold Medal game with the North team. The South team was the favorite, largely on the basis of O'Neal's past performances in the Olympic series. He had scored 89 points in the first three games.

The game was a nail-biter, with the South team pulling out the win in the final seconds, 121–120, before a crowd of 10,434 at Williams Arena. Shaq had an off night, scoring only 9 points before fouling out. Surprisingly, he drew most of the postgame attention despite the fact that the clear star of the game was Penny Hardaway, who scored 21 points for the South team. Scoring was not what pleased Hardaway the most, though.

"We won the Gold Medal game for the South," he recalled. "I gave Shaquille a no-look pass on the break. He tore down the rim. Everyone said. 'Oooooo.' I do passing best. I can see everything happening on the floor."

Newspaper accounts the following day ignored Hardaway but praised O'Neal for his 55 rebounds and 27 blocked shots in the tournament. This didn't bother Hardaway; he had come to Minneapolis to prove he could play with some of the best young players in America, even though he couldn't join them for further competition in 1990. (He still had to sit out that Prop 48 year at Memphis State.) In the end, even Coach Brown acknowledged his talent in a private conversation with Anfernee Hardaway.

Williams Arena had become to him a proving ground. He passed the test with flying colors, but the most difficult year in his young life lay ahead.

At college, Hardaway took 17 credits in his first semester, majoring in elementary education, and achieved a grade point average of close to 3.0 (a B average). He registered for 15 more credits the following semester. Prop 48 guidelines state that, for eventual participation in sports, successful completion of 24 credits per year is required. By taking more credits than necessary, Hardaway was out to show that the stereotype of "dumb jock" did not apply to him.

Away from class, he made good use of the school's various gymnasium facilities. The Mid-South Coliseum was his favorite. He would arrive alone early in the morning, while the rest of the campus slept, and shoot a seemingly endless string of jump shots.

He made very few friends that first year. "People think I'm dumb," he told a reporter "Even the brothers from the 'hood' do it, too. A guy once said, 'Oh, yeah, you're that dumb ballplayer.' He's known for selling cocaine. But he thinks I'm the dumb one." The mean streets of Memphis finally caught up with Hardaway in his freshmen year at college, providing yet another obstacle in his path.

In April 1991, Hardaway was on his way to recording the highest scholastic grade point average of any Memphis State student athlete out for basketball (even though he was not a member of the team). One day, he and a friend were casually standing in front of the Memphis home of Hardaway's cousin, LaMarcus Golden. Suddenly, a car pulled up next to them, and four men jumped out.

It soon became apparent that the men carried weapons and that this was a robbery. Rather than risk what could happen if they resisted, Hardaway and his friend emptied their wallets. Hardaway also handed over his watch, a gold rope necklace, and an AAU championship ring that he had won in 1988 as a member of the Memphis YMCA seventeen-and-under team.

As the thieves ran off, one of their guns accidentally went off, and a bullet ricocheted off the pavement and struck Hardaway. The bullet broke three bones in his foot.

Hardaway was then forced to lie face down on the pavement as another robber pressed a revolver against his neck. "I kept thinking," Hardaway said, "that he's going to shoot me in the back or in the head. I'm glad to be alive today. They knew we had seen their faces, and I thought they would go ahead and just kill us." Seconds seemed like hours. After what seemed like a very long time, something or somebody caused the robbers to run away. They were never caught.

What more could happen to Hardaway? He already had faced the humiliation of not being allowed to play college basketball for one year because of his poor grades. Now he had been shot in front of his own cousin's house. Hardaway easily could have called it quits right there; he could have abandoned sports and a college education. Many others would have done just that—not Anfernee Hardaway.

He spent months with a cast on his foot. The bullet couldn't be removed until that November, after practice had started for his first intercollegiate athletic season.

In his first game as a sophomore in 1991, Hardaway scored 18 points, including a three-pointer that sent the game into overtime. He also hauled in 15 rebounds, dished out 6 assists, blocked 4 shots, and came up with 4 steals. The game was significant for other reasons too. It was the first one played in the Pyramid, one of America's most striking new arenas. The Memphis State Tigers began play at the new facility after occupying the Mid-South Coliseum for twenty-seven years. The $65 million pyramid-shaped arena is covered with 6.9 acres of stainless steel and stands 321 feet high on the east bank of the Mississippi River. The Pyramid seats 20,142 people.

Hardaway's coach, Larry Finch, feared opening night jitters for his star player. "It's a different world when you're coming out to play before 20,000 screaming people." Finch soon learned that crowds didn't bother Hardaway at all.

In fact, the debut of both Hardaway and the new building caused *Sports Illustrated* to observe: "Elvis had Graceland. Anfernee has the Pyramid."

Things were looking up for the hometown guy. In the next few home games, he turned the Pyramid into the "Tomb of Doom" for Memphis opponents. Tickets to games at the new arena were hard to come by after Hardaway's debut, and the team responded to crowd affection by going 12–4 at home in his first season. On January 8, 1992, Hardaway scored 26 points to lead his team past a powerful Missouri team, 89–78. A month later, he led Memphis State past rival Arkansas, 92–88, with 15 points, 8 rebounds, and 10 assists.

Arkansas coach Nolan Richardson, who had recruited Hardaway and nearly had succeeded in getting him to come to

Memphis State's awesome 20,142-seat arena, the Pyramid, is where Hardaway played his first game as a collegian. *Sports Illustrated* commented, "Elvis had Graceland. Anfernee has the Pyramid."

Fayetteville, observed; "Hardaway can make the big shot to beat you, the great pass to create a play, and he will make the tough free throws."

In a 77–64 win over Southwestern Louisiana, Hardaway had 4 slam dunks on the way to a 17-point, 8-rebound, 6-assist performance. "That felt good," he said afterward. "I have always said that I will do whatever it takes to help the team win."

Memphis State continued to win, fooling the experts who had predicted a mediocre season for the Tigers. What the experts hadn't anticipated was the outstanding play of Hardaway, who was rapidly becoming one of the best guards in college basketball.

Hardaway had 22 points, 11 rebounds, and 9 assists, as the Tigers defeated DePaul, 95–75. Even Magic Johnson took

22

notice. He said, "He's a great player who can do it all; scoring, passing, whatever. When I saw him I thought I was looking in a mirror; he reminds me of myself so much." Actually, Sonny Vaccaro had once compared Hardaway to Magic Johnson.

The regular season ended with Memphis posting a mark of 18 wins and 9 losses. In the Great Midwest Conference Tournament, the Tigers knocked off Alabama-Birmingham and DePaul before losing in the finals to Cincinnati, 75–63.

The team's losses, while hard to take, were often the result of fellow players' inability to handle Hardaway's bullet passes. It had taken most of the year for Hardaway and his teammates to become used to each other.

Despite the Cincinnati defeat, an invitation to the NCAA tournament was extended to Coach Finch, who accepted on behalf of his team. "Now the real season begins," he exclaimed. Memphis State drew Pepperdine in the first round of the sixty-four-team tournament and defeated the Waves, 80–70, in Milwaukee. Hardaway led the team with 21 points, 8 rebounds, and 7 assists.

Next came Arkansas, anxious to avenge the earlier defeat at the hands of the Tigers. Once again, Memphis State triumphed, 82–80, and advanced to the next round in Kansas City.

By now, Hardaway and his teammates were operating in sync. "It was amazing," Finch said, "the year he's having after sitting out as long as he did. Hardaway can do it all and is making passes where I turn around and mumble to myself, because I have no idea how he saw the open player. And the players on the bench are laughing at me. 'Coach, he does that all the time,' they'll say to me."

Georgia Tech of the Atlantic Coast Conference (ACC) was waiting for the Tigers in Kansas City. Memphis State was the clear underdog, and it looked like the Tigers' season was over when Tech's Matt Geiger completed a three-point play

Superscout Sonny Vaccaro said Hardaway's ability and performance on the court reminded him of the L.A. Lakers' all-time great Magic Johnson.

with 36 seconds left in the game to give the Yellow Jackets a 74–70 lead. MSU battled back, and with 11 seconds remaining, Billy Smith poured in a jump shot to tie the game and send it to overtime. In the extra period, Memphis State took its first lead of the game with 1:41 left to play when Tony Madlock dropped in a pair of free throws. The Tigers hung on for a heart-stopping 83–79 victory and advanced to the next round.

Almost overlooked in the aftermath of the Georgia Tech victory was the fact that Hardaway came close to having his best game as a collegian that night in Kansas City. In addition to scoring 24 points against the Yellow Jackets, he poured in a season-high 5 three-pointers, most from NBA range. He also had 7 assists.

Amazingly, out of sixty-four teams in the tournament field, Memphis State was again paired against the arch-rival Cincinnati Bearcats for the right to advance to the 1992 Final

Four in Minneapolis. The Bearcats were riding a nine-game winning streak and had breezed through their first three NCAA tournament games.

The Tigers played their best ball in the first 10 minutes of the game and took a 23–21 lead. Unfortunately, Hardaway picked up his third foul on a questionable call and headed to the bench. From that point, Memphis State lost momentum and eventually fell to Cincinnati, 88–57.

"I'm elated we were in the final eight," Finch said, "and had an opportunity at the Final Four. We'll see if we can knock on the door again next year and maybe it will open."

Hardaway was showered with postseason awards including honorable mention Associated Press All-American, Great Midwest Conference Most Valuable Player, and *Basketball Times'* Newcomer of the Year.

He easily led his team in scoring, assists, and steals, and he set a school record with 69 three-point baskets. He had scored 20 or more points in 14 games in his first season and hit double figures in 31 of 34 games. More importantly, he became the first player in Memphis State history to score at least 500 points, grab 200 rebounds, hand out 150 assists, and make 70 steals in a single season. He was also picked to play for the U.S.A. Development Team that was set to practice against the Olympic Dream Team that year.

Of all the honors he received that year, though, the one that meant the most was the award for attaining the Memphis State basketball team's top grade point average for the 1992 spring semester. He had a 3.2 grade point average (B+) in five classes. "Since coming to Memphis State," exclaimed sports information director Mark Owens, "Anfernee Hardaway has been the model student athlete."

"I always knew in my heart I could do it," Hardaway told Owens. "I just messed up at Treadwell High School. All through elementary school, I was a straight-A student. But in junior high school, I just stopped doing the work because I was playing basketball. When I got to college, I figured it was time to apply my ability in the classroom."

Anfernee earned a pair of As, two Bs, and a C—all in a hectic period of postseason play for the Tigers when the team was away from Memphis for long periods of time.

Hardaway was out to convince everyone that he was no dummy. His classroom work that semester silenced his academic critics. There were other critics, however, who questioned his play on the basketball court. "He needs to improve his shooting," one said. These critics then looked at Penny's performance against the Olympic Dream Team that spring and fell silent. Basketball has been an Olympic sport since 1936. A "dream team" of professional basketball players was selected to represent the United States in the 1992 Olympics. Hardaway was named to an eight-man development squad that was chosen to work out against the Dream Team. Hardaway not only held his own against the best basketball players in the world, he outplayed some of them.

He said later that he didn't know how many points he scored in the workouts because he was concentrating on his defensive play. "I wanted to prove myself defensively against the best," he told *Street & Smith's Basketball Magazine*. "I think that's what it takes to get to the next level. I learned I have to get stronger and smarter. It helped me so much just to watch those guys. Larry Bird taught me that it's not all strength and height. In this game, it's smartness too."

Hardaway's play impressed other Olympic Team members. "Anfernee Hardaway," said 1992 Olympian Scottie Pippen, "has a bright future ahead in the National Basketball Association." Hardaway recalled that the great Larry Bird had called him Mr. Defense. In scrimmages, he was able to take the Olympians off their dribble, and he easily stole the ball from Magic Johnson, John Stockton, Charles Barkley, and even Michael Jordan.

As a scorer during his first year of play in college, Hardaway had received no recognition for outstanding defensive play. "Coming to the Olympic camp I was not known for my defense," Hardaway recalled. "But I was able to step up and play good defense against the world's best players," he said proudly. Dream Team coach Chuck Daly was impressed: "He has the athletic and basketball ability to be a first-round pick in the NBA. I particularly liked his ability to swing to different positions. This is a very valuable asset in today's game of basketball."

Bird recalled that Hardaway put the Dream Team to the test in every day of practice. "He is such a versatile athlete and plays both ends of the court extremely hard. He did a super job and helped us prepare for winning the Gold Medal." Patrick Ewing said, "I look forward to playing against him in the NBA one day in the future."

Hardaway and his Memphis State teammates were sky-high as the 1991–92 season began. The team was riding the crest of the wave that had brought them to NCAA prominence the season before. A national championship seemed possible.

Chapter 3

Mention the name Larry Finch anywhere around the city of Memphis and the first thing most natives think of is winning basketball. From his days as a player at Memphis State, through the period when he was an assistant coach, to his present position as head coach, Finch has been a major part of the success that has made Memphis State successful.

"People forget how young a team we were last season," Coach Finch said. "But this year, we should be a more mature and experienced group. At least I hope we are."

The Tigers were anchored by a strong starting lineup that included the All-American Hardaway, David Vaughn, Billy Smith, and Anthony Douglas. After surprising everyone in the NCAA tournament, the Tigers had the city of Memphis eager for another chance at the Final Four.

By now, the intercollegiate basketball world outside Memphis recognized Hardaway's excellence. He could do it all on the basketball court—score, pass, rebound, block shots, make timely steals, and bring Pyramid crowds to their feet with electrifying slam dunks. He also could make at least one

Mention the name "Larry Finch" (on the left, next to Hardaway) in Memphis, and people will think of only one thing—winning basketball.

play every game that would leave basketball fans, at home or on the road, shaking their heads in total amazement. One such play during the previous season was against Southwestern Louisiana, when Tiger Tony Madlock grabbed a rebound, and threw the ball nearly the length of the court. Hardaway watched the ball bounce by the free throw line, and, in one motion, caught it on its upward flight and slammed it home. Those who were there would never forget that moment.

That was last season, though. The fans expected more in the 1992–93 season, Hardaway's junior year at Memphis State. "We have one of the toughest nonconference schedules of any college basketball team," warned Coach Finch, who called attention to season-opening road games at Arkansas and Tennessee. "And the Great Midwest Conference will be awesome."

Memphis fans easily ignored Finch's warning, even

knowing that hated Arkansas would be the Tigers' first opponent. Razorback coach Nolan Richardson hadn't forgotten his team's two losses to Memphis State in the previous season, and he was out for revenge.

The Arkansas game began, and the Tigers' star six-foot-nine-inch power forward David Vaughn, son of a former NBA player and nephew of Coach Finch, had played only twenty-one minutes against Arkansas when he was lost for the season.

Memphis State had the Razorbacks down by 20 points and was coasting when Vaughn suffered a partially torn anterior cruciate ligament in his left knee. Interior cruciate injuries are among the most painful and damaging in sports. Once the X rays were in, the word was out. David Vaughn would have to sit out the entire 1992–93 season. Although Hardaway went on to score 27 points, pull down 7 rebounds, and distribute 6 assists, the Tigers fell to Arkansas, 81–76. "You don't replace David Vaughn," Finch said sadly. "We have to go back to the drawing board."

David Vaughn, Hardaway's co-star at Memphis State, was lost for the 1992–93 season after only playing twenty-one minutes against Arkansas in the season-opening game.

Four days later, Memphis State was in Knoxville, playing cross-state rival Tennessee in the team's first game without Vaughn. The Tigers trailed for most of the game and seemed lifeless. The Volunteers easily defeated Memphis State, 70–59. Hardaway finished with 15 points, 11 rebounds, and 8 assists. "Things will be different," he vowed afterward, "when we get back to our house, the Pyramid."

At the Pyramid, twenty-first-ranked Tulane University was waiting for the Tigers. After a seesaw battle for most of the game, Tulane forged ahead by 10 points with 7 minutes left to play, and the home crowd was less than enthusiastic. What was wrong with the Tigers?

Memphis State cut the Tulane lead to 4 points at 86–82 with only 37 seconds left in the game. Hardaway took the ball across midcourt, paused beyond NBA three-point distance, and fired. The ball swished through the net. Now 28 seconds showed on the clock. Tulane missed a pair of free throws, and the Tigers had one more shot at victory. Hardaway was double-teamed, so he fed the ball to Anthony Douglas with five seconds left. Douglas drove the lane and put up a shot. The ball rolled off the rim, and Tulane won.

The losses to Arkansas and Tennessee had been easier to take, but losing at home to Tulane was something else. The fans slowly filed out of the Pyramid. Memphis State was 0–3. What was happening? Coach Finch remained positive. "I think we are improving," he said, "especially in our passing game. There is no need to panic."

Two nights later, the fans were willing to believe Finch. Southwestern Louisiana came to the Pyramid and left 91–85 losers. Hardaway led the way with 23 points, 8 rebounds, and 8 assists. The team took the next week off for final examinations. The opportunity to concentrate on classroom work and to forget basketball seemed to have a relaxing effect on team members. Memphis State returned from exams and posted an 81–78 win over the Jackson State Tigers. Hardaway tossed 27 points in the victory.

The team then headed west—far, far west—all the way to Hawaii to compete in the annual Maui Invitational. The Tigers drew host team, Chaminade, in the opening game. The Silver Swords, who were notorious for pulling upsets on their home floor, planned to defeat Memphis easily. Although the Tigers trailed early, Hardaway decided to take matters into his own hands and took more shots than usual. The result was a career-high 33 points for Hardaway and a 64–56 victory for his team.

Memphis State drew Brigham Young in the next round of the invitational tournament. The game was remembered not for its outcome, but for a single incredible play by Anfernee Hardaway. In Hawaii, they still marvel over what he did that night. Midway through the game, he drove toward the basket on the baseline and came up against a Brigham Young defender. What happened next defies description. Somehow Hardaway was able to leap clear over the defender and score a basket. No one in attendance that night had ever seen anything like it. The following day, Hardaway's leap was all anyone would talk about. Conveniently ignored was the fact that Brigham Young had defeated Memphis State, 73–67. Hardaway took no special pride in his extraordinary move to the basket, which had set tongues wagging. "He hates to lose," his coach observed afterward.

Hardaway tasted victory the following night when he grabbed 8 rebounds and scored 20 points to help the Tigers defeat Louisiana State, 70–66. This was a frail Louisiana State bunch, however, and most definitely not the same team as it had been the previous season. That team was led by Shaquille

O'Neal, who now was a star in the National Basketball Association with the Orlando Magic.

Hardaway's dream had always been to play professional basketball. Seeing his old Olympic Festival teammate excelling in the pros heightened Hardaway's desire. Was he ready for the NBA, though?

Marty Blake, the NBA director of scouting, had said he thought Hardaway should wait another year before thinking about joining the league. Blake and others felt that Hardaway's slight build would work against him. He needed another year of college competition to build some muscle. Hardaway was also lacking in physical stamina.

Hardaway told everyone that he wouldn't talk about the NBA until the Memphis State season was over. Getting back to the NCAA tournament was his most immediate goal.

Before leaving Hawaii, Hardaway was named co-Most Valuable Player in the Maui Invitational, along with Bobby Hurley of Duke. Hardaway, tourney officials noted, had scored 90 points in his three tournament games. Duke, however, had won the tournament, defeating Brigham Young, 89–66, in the championship game.

Memphis State returned to the Pyramid, and won the fifth game of the season by defeating a stubborn Robert Morris team, 78–63, after trailing at halftime. The Tigers made only 10 of 31 shots in the first half, but, after an inspiring halftime speech by Finch, Hardaway took charge of the game, finishing with 25 points, 7 assists, and 6 rebounds.

Minnesota was next on the schedule. Because Memphis State had played the Golden Gophers at home the previous season (and won, 65–62), the rematch was scheduled for Williams Arena in Minneapolis. Hardaway looked on the game as a homecoming of sorts; Williams Arena had been the place where he had proved he could hold his own in competition with the best during the Olympic Festival.

When he had played in Minneapolis before, he had, for the most part, been ignored by the local press. Now he was returning to the city as an All-American, and members of the sports media stood in line to speak with him.

The game, he told reporters, was of special importance. His team had been struggling, and this was an opportunity to prove their worth on the road against an opponent from the Big Ten Conference.

The game started with Memphis State attacking the basket. The basketball became a blur as Hardaway raced at full speed, gracefully pushing the ball ahead of him. A pair of gold-shirted defenders stood before him, their arms extended. Hardaway slipped between them and left his feet just beyond the foul line, soaring sideways through the air with the ball held high. Amazingly, he changed direction in midair to face the basket. He then jammed the ball through for 2 points. The home crowd fell silent. Most had never seen a human being make such a move with a basketball. Slowly, one by one, they rose to their feet, shouting and applauding.

Two hours later, the freezing temperature and icy winds penetrated Hardaway's jacket like a knife. It was New Year's Eve, but it was 12° below zero outside, and no one in his group felt like celebrating. Despite their awesome beginning, the Tigers had gone on to lose to Minnesota, 70–55.

Hardaway entered the game making exactly 50 percent of his field goal attempts (77 for 154) in 9 previous games. Against Minnesota, he made just 10 out of 25. He had only 3 assists, and even worse, he turned the ball over to the opposition 5 times.

A second-string Minnesota guard named Nate Tubbs had been assigned to watch Hardaway and had hung on him all night, forcing Hardaway off his usual game. As a result, Hardaway started to force his shots. More importantly, the pesky Tubbs had bothered Penny enough to keep him from passing the ball to teammates. Because of this, no other Memphis State player had scored more than 7 points. Even the spectacular basket that aroused the home crowd was tainted because a pair of teammates had open lanes to the hoop. Instead of passing the ball, Hardaway kept it for himself and drove the lane.

"More was expected of Memphis State this season," observed Patrick Reusse, sportswriter for the *Minneapolis Star Tribune*. He noted that the Tigers were rated number 7 in the Associated Press preseason poll.

"Hardaway is in constant motion on the court, but he was only 4 for 12 in three-point attempts last night." Reusse did observe that the three he did make were a "minimum of five feet beyond" the three-point line.

On the trip back to Memphis, Anfernee was deeply depressed. He wondered what could be done to turn things around. He told the coach he had shot the ball too much against Minnesota. He wanted things to be different in 1993. "It's frustrating," he said over and over again.

Back in Memphis, the team meeting cleared the air. Film of the game was reviewed. There was Hardaway on the screen, pulling up at least five feet outside the NBA three-point line and firing a shot. The ball hit nothing but net. Whistles of appreciation were heard in the darkened room, but Hardaway could only bury his head and recall the eight similar shots that missed the mark in Minneapolis.

As the film ended, Hardaway stood up and tearfully told the group he would play unselfishly in the future. "Penny was upset," remembered Finch, "but he's a natural leader." The coach was glad to see his star asserting himself. "He's like the Pied Piper around here. All the things Penny has gone through

Hardaway scored 30 points against Minnesota on New Year's Eve in Minneapolis, but was closely guarded by Nate Tubbs of the Gophers (left).

could have made him bitter. Instead, they have made him fight that much harder to overcome adversity. He's truly a special person. And one thing you are going to find out is that he is a totally unselfish basketball player." The vote of confidence from his coach was all Hardaway needed.

Basketball fans enjoy tracking individual accomplishments, especially when a player scores, rebounds, makes assists, blocks shots, or steals the ball more than 10 times in a game. If, in a single game, he gets more than 10 in two categories, it is called a double-double. If he does this for three categories, it's a triple-double. No basketball player in Memphis State history had ever recorded a triple-double—not until January 4, 1993.

In a win over Georgia State, Hardaway had 21 points, 15 rebounds, and, most importantly, 14 assists—a triple-double. He also had 4 steals, 2 blocked shots, and 5 slam dunks. It was an astonishing performance that placed him in the forefront of a line of Memphis State basketball greats that includes All-Americans Win Wilfong, Keith Lee, Hardaway's high school teammate Elliott Perry, and current coach Larry Finch.

Amazingly, Hardaway rang up his second straight triple double against Vanderbilt University.

No sooner had the dust settled on that performance than Hardaway was at it again. This time he was up against Vanderbilt, a team ranked 18th-best in the nation. Amazingly, Hardaway rang up his second straight triple-double, with 26 points, 12 rebounds, and 10 assists. More important to Hardaway, Memphis State won, 84–78. The Tigers were back.

On January 9, Memphis State traveled to Chicago to take on their Great Midwest Conference rival DePaul. Before the game, Windy City reporters quickly noted that Hardaway had a grim, determined look about him. For those accustomed to his easy smile and quick conversation, this represented a startling change.

Hardaway was a man on a mission, out to prove that he was a complete basketball player. Nothing would stand in his way. When the game ended, the scoreboard read: Memphis State 95, DePaul 93. Hardaway had scored 35 points and pulled down 15 rebounds to pace the Tigers past the Blue Demons to the team's third consecutive victory.

More significantly, the entire sporting world took notice of Hardaway during the Tigers' three-game run against Georgia State, Vanderbilt, and DePaul.

Sports Illustrated named Hardaway its Player of the Week, reporting that he had a triple-double average of 27.3 points, 14 rebounds, and 10 assists in the three games. He was named Great Midwest Conference Player of the Week, and the ESPN television network proclaimed him National Player of the Week. Arkansas coach Nolan Richardson observed that if you "roll Larry Bird, Magic Johnson, and Michael Jordan together, you get Penny Hardaway."

Memphis State was on a roll. Southeastern Louisiana fell, 109–58, then Tennessee Tech, 101–71. In the Tennessee Tech game, Hardaway did something unbelievable.

While on defense, he instinctively slapped the ball away from a dribbling opponent and raced after it toward his team's basket. He caught up with the ball, faced the basket, then surprised everyone by lobbing the ball in the air. The move was mystifying because no other player was close to him. He then jumped up, snatched the ball in midair, and dunked it through the hoop. The audience rose to its feet as one, and the subsequent cheers and applause created a noise that rivaled the sound of jet airplane taking off.

When DePaul came to Memphis in a rematch of the January 9 game, reporter Lynn Zinser of the *Commercial Appeal* noted that a change had come over Hardaway in the Tigers' ten previous games. Hardaway, he noted, previously wore a "telling, tired look." He was carrying the weight of the team squarely on his shoulders.

Now, the new Hardaway laughed easily and joked with reporters. He granted interviews, took all phone calls from reporters, and traded quips with Dick Vitale and other representatives of the national television networks.

"It's great to see my team come in and take up the scoring when I'm not scoring," Hardaway told Zinser. "When teams double-team me, that's going to leave somebody open, and they're taking advantage of it now. Earlier in the year, they didn't know how to react."

Teammate Kelvin Allen observed that the team was helping to take the pressure off Hardaway. This allowed him to control the flow of the game and stop attempting to do everything himself. He now could direct the flow of play and position teammates in the best place to score. Against DePaul, Hardaway scored only 12 points, but he grabbed rebounds and distributed 6 assists. Memphis State won easily, 79–57. The team was on a five-game winning streak and sported a 16–7 win-loss record.

More importantly, the team had discovered the value of playing sound defense. The team's last ten opponents shot a collective 36 percent from the field, hardly an impressive mark for them. It would be nice to report that Memphis State went from there to capture the conference title and advance to the NCAA Final Four. But it was not to be. The team had overcome the earlier injury to David Vaughn, but another key player, guard Sidney Coles, went down with a hairline fracture to his left fibula. This is the smaller of the two bones below the knee. Memphis State lost two of their next three games.

Despite the adversity, the Tigers won two of their last three regular season games, including a 68–63 win over 20th-ranked Marquette, and made it to the finals of the Great Midwest Conference Tournament before falling to Cincinnati in the title game, 77–72.

Memphis State had a 20–11 win-loss record and was invited to the NCAA tournament for the fourteenth time in school history. The Tigers were named to face Western Kentucky in the opening round of the sixty-four team tournament in Orlando, Florida, on March 18, 1993.

No one knew it at the time, but this was to be Hardaway's last college basketball game.

Chapter 4

All his life, Anfernee Hardaway has struggled to climb to the next level of competition. For him, there was only one level remaining—the National Basketball Association. Was he ready?

Deep in his heart he believed the time had come. True, he had another year of eligibility left at Memphis State, but he knew he had learned all he could at the collegiate level. Another year would have taught him nothing new and would cause him to risk an injury that could jeopardize his professional career.

He did not go out a winner at Memphis State, but, then, only one NCAA tournament team goes through the season without suffering a defeat in its last game. Sixty-three of the sixty-four teams in the tournament field must lose before a champion is crowned. For Hardaway, that defeat came early. His Memphis State Tigers didn't make it past the first round of the tournament.

Coach Finch decided to allow the team to stay in Orlando and visit Disney World. The team arrived at the theme park around noon, and most of the players headed straight for the

Space Mountain roller coaster. The following day, the Tigers went to Universal Studios. Orlando, Hardaway learned, might be a good place to live.

On March 31, 1993, the sports information department of Memphis State University called a press conference. Anfernee Hardaway, the best basketball player ever to wear Tiger blue and gray, was going to enter the 1993 National Basketball Association draft on June 30. The official announcement said that Hardaway was skipping his senior season in the best interests of his family and himself. The press conference was held in the lobby of the Athletic Office Building. Now it was done. All that was left was waiting to see which NBA team would draft him.

By the luck of the draw, the Orlando Magic were selected in the NBA lottery to have the first pick in the upcoming player draft. Now, Hardaway thought, if only Orlando would pick me!

In the meantime, Hardaway was voted a first-team

Hardaway, the best player ever to wear a Memphis State uniform, decided to enter the NBA draft a year before his collegiate eligibility was up.

All-American by the Associated Press. Joining him on the first team were Chris Webber, Bobby Hurley, Calbert Cheaney, and Jamal Mashburn.

This was the first of many postseason honors. He was one of the top five vote-getters on the ESPN John Wooden All-America team. He also was selected as a finalist for the RCA Player of the Year award won by Calbert Cheaney. United Press International, the U.S. Basketball Writers Association, and the National Association of Basketball Coaches also placed Hardaway on their first-string All-American teams.

Orlando Magic general manager and chief operating officer Pat Williams said that while he was very impressed with Hardaway, Michigan's Chris Webber interested him even more.

When Webber arrived in Orlando for a predraft workout at the expense of the Orlando team, he was whisked away from the airport, placed in a special team limo, wined and dined, and taken to meet reporters. When it came time for Hardaway's workout, no one was waiting for him at the airport. He hitched a ride with a television cameraman, and the two stopped for breakfast. Magic team officials appeared to be impressed by Hardaway's workout in Orlando, but they made no promises.

On June 12, a public pep rally was held in Memphis with Hardaway as the main attraction. At the Mall of Memphis, he announced an antidrug campaign called "Be Drug Free." He then filmed a series of radio and television spots promoting the program.

A Paramount Pictures representative named Dan Parada called Hardaway and asked if he would be interested in appearing in an upcoming basketball movie, *Blue Chips*, starring Nick Nolte. Hardaway was lukewarm about the idea until he heard that his friend Shaquille O'Neal was part of the project. Hardaway was told he would be in a few scenes with O'Neal if he agreed to do the movie.

A formal offer from Paramount was made, and Hardaway signed on to play actress Alfre Woodard's son in the movie. He would take on the role of a star high school athlete whose family was concerned about his well-being at a major university. The role sounded familiar to Hardaway, and he believed it would not be hard to perform. Besides he would have a chance to work out with his old Olympic Festival teammate O'Neal.

Hardaway had put his desire to play for Orlando on hold for his career as an antidrug spokesperson and movie actor, so he was surprised to receive an urgent request from the Magic. Pat Williams and other team officials wanted another look at him. This was June 29, the night before the draft, so something definitely was in the air.

Before the draft, any league team is free to try out, at their whim, players believed to have NBA potential. Sometimes an initial visit (such as Hardaway's) is not enough to decide whether a player fits into a team's long-range planning. Players are then invited back for additional workouts. What was somewhat unusual about Hardaway's situation was that Orlando waited until the day before the draft for a second look at him. Hardaway could have turned down the invitation to display his talents, but he did not. The second workout was all Orlando needed to justify trading their original first pick, Webber, for Hardaway.

Hardaway turned in a incredible ninety-minute performance, making all manner of dunk shots, behind-the-back passes, and three-point shots. Those in attendance were spellbound. Later it was revealed that the Magic master plan had been to draft Webber, who would fill a hole at power forward for Orlando, until Hardaway's workout took place. The workout changed everything. Now the Magic wanted Hardaway, not Webber. In less than twenty-four hours, the thinking of Williams and the members of the front office of the Magic had been reversed. A last-minute trade was then worked out with the Golden State Warriors, the team that held the third pick in the NBA draft. The teams swapped first-round draft picks, and the Magic also received the Warriors' first-round picks for 1996, 1998, and 2000. As a result, Chris Webber went to Golden State and Penny Hardaway went to Orlando.

"Hardaway," said Dick DeVos, the Magic's president, describing the workout the day before, "was absolutely spectacular. He impressed everyone in the building and practically everyone within a half-mile."

Boston Globe writer Bob Ryan observed: "Anfernee Hardaway and Shaquille O'Neal will be in the 1990s what Kareem Abdul-Jabbar and Magic Johnson were in the 1980s."

Back in Orlando, the team's fans were not so optimistic. More than eight thousand had gathered for a draft night celebration. When the trade was announced, the majority of those in attendance reacted by booing. They wanted, and expected to get, Chris Webber. Anfernee Hardaway would have to win them over.

Shaquille O'Neal instantly knew that his team had made the right choice. "I can tell you," he said, "that with Hardaway, you're going to see a lot more show time. He can do more things with a basketball that will make us a better, more fun team to watch. He's the real deal." O'Neal then joined Hardaway on the set of *Blue Chips*, which was filmed that summer. The movie was released six months later and received the critics' acclaim. Hardaway, it seemed, was as good an actor as he was a ballplayer. "Making the movie was a great experience for me," he remarked. "I think it's a great movie, too."

As his first NBA season approached, Hardaway told all who would listen of his respect for O'Neal. He said he tried not to worry about living up to anyone else's expectations himself, but he did know that Shaq was a great ballplayer, possibly the best center in basketball history. O'Neal, according to Hardaway, was so big, strong, and powerful that anyone would have a hard time stopping him. As for himself, Hardaway said that he just had to go out, play hard in every game, and try to use all of his talents.

He hired sports agents Kevin and Carl Poston to work out a contract for him with the Magic. The negotiations proved to be long and drawn-out. "We like to get what the market thinks a player is worth," Carl Poston explained. NBA teams

When he first arrived in Orlando to play for the Magic, Hardaway (with ball) received a chilly reception.

traditionally prefer to pay a player a salary that is about the same as the salaries of other players.

Hardaway's image in Orlando suffered because his agents and the Magic could not agree on contract terms. In Memphis, he was extremely popular, but in Orlando his name was mud. "Negotiation is an art," said Carl Poston, but Magic fans were not impressed. Faithful Orlando supporters had been counting on getting Chris Webber. Now Webber's replacement was refusing to sign a Magic contract.

Chapter 5

At a special news conference in Orlando it was announced by general manager Williams and the Poston brothers that Hardaway would sign a thirteen-year contract for $68 million, a sum larger than any ever paid to a player selected third in the NBA draft. Orlando fans could not believe that their team was willing to part with so much money for a slender point guard who had never played in an NBA game.

The problem the Magic had faced was how to sign Hardaway when it had little room under the NBA salary cap. The NBA allows each team only so much money to spend on players. Orlando had already spent nearly all that the team was allowed. One of the moves the team made was to allow Hardaway to renegotiate his contract after his first season. Another was to release Magic power forward Brian Williams. The choice did not sit well with Orlando fans. Williams eventually went on to star for the Denver Nuggets.

The fans were in a foul mood, especially after the first few times Hardaway played at home. His performance was tentative and uneven. After an exhibition game with Miami, he was selected the game's Best Substitute. The crowd booed the selection. Orlando coach Brian Hill told Hardaway to ignore the boos. In time, the fans would come to appreciate him for his many talents.

Hardaway was bewildered. He had been granted his wish to play with his favorite NBA team, but now it seemed that few in Orlando wanted him there. In Memphis, he was a king, but Memphis had no NBA team.

This poor reception was simply another obstacle thrown in his path. Someone had once told him that what doesn't kill you will make you stronger. Penny knew this to be true, because everything bad that had happened to him before had only made him fight harder. He gritted his teeth and vowed to win the Magic fans over.

The Orlando fans stayed on his back until November 23, 1993—the day the Golden State Warriors made their only visit that season to Orlando Arena. Golden State brought with them their young star power forward Chris Webber, the man Magic fans felt should have been theirs.

The one thing Hardaway has been consistently able to do throughout his career is to rise to a challenge. Without a doubt, this was a major challenge. The fans of Orlando would have a chance to compare him with Chris Webber. He would not disappoint them.

Hardaway played his best game as a professional. He scored 23 points and grabbed 8 rebounds in a 120–107 Orlando win. Webber played well, too, taking 10 rebounds and scoring 13, but his efforts couldn't carry the team. When the final whistle sounded, Hardaway was rewarded with a standing ovation.

More significantly, a group of Hardaway's newfound Orlando fans held a banner they had made earlier in the day.

The banner read: "WE PICKED THE RIGHT ONE BABY!" Hardaway truly had become the "right one" for the Magic.

Selena Roberts of the *Orlando Sentinel* reported that from the start, "Hardaway showed himself to be an intense professional who hates to lose and loves the game of basketball. Those are the markings of a leader," she wrote. Hardaway told Roberts that he probably wouldn't be taking as many shots as before, "because I'm being asked to help distribute the ball. We have other shooters on the floor."

Hardaway's counterpart at guard, veteran Scott Skiles, praised the rookie's ability to create plays and noted that he had the potential to be an everyday point guard. The battle-worn Skiles, however, had been selected by Coach Hill to be the Magic's starting point guard.

For the time being, Hardaway would have to settle for the shooting guard spot in the lineup. He said he was happy with the assignment. Later, though, he admitted that he had wanted to play point guard from the opening tip-off of Orlando's first exhibition game.

In the early months of the 1993–94 season, Hardaway played the shooting guard position. He struggled at first, but in a January 10 game against that season's eventual NBA champion Houston Rockets, Penny and Shaq scored 28 points apiece, and the Magic used a 13–0 fourth-quarter run to break open a close game and win by 115–110.

On January 26 at Charlotte, Penny poured in 32 points and just missed a triple-double with 9 assists and 9 rebounds. The Magic hit 20 of 24 shots in the fourth quarter against the Hornets to turn a 6-point lead entering the period into a 27-point advantage. Hardaway wasn't the only Orlando player to go on a scoring binge that night. O'Neal had 36 points, and forward Nick Anderson had 29 points.

Hardaway's confidence level was at its highest, and Coach

Penny Hardaway poured in 32 points during the game against the Rockets on January 26. His outstanding perform-ance early in his rookie season earned him the position of starting point guard.

Hill decided to reward him with the point guard position. Even the Magic's former point guard, Scott Skiles, agreed Hardaway was ready to take the job. (The Magic had traded Skiles that summer.)

Few NBA rookies have been placed under the pressure that came with Hardaway's first start at point guard. The opponent was the division-leading New York Knicks, on a Sunday afternoon in Madison Square Garden, before a national television audience. Hardaway admitted to having jitters before the game. When the time came for him to lace up his shoes, though, he knew he was ready.

The game was a close, defensive struggle, with New York posting a 77–73 lead with only 4.5 minutes left to play. Orlando seemed ready to take control when Shaq was called for a questionable offensive foul for backing into Knicks center Patrick Ewing. New York's Charles Smith then drove past O'Neal and was fouled. Smith made both free throws, Shaq missed a scoop shot, the Knicks rebounded, and John Starks raced up the floor, pulled up for a three-pointer, and sank the shot. At that point, New York led by 9, and they went on to win, 95 to 77.

Hardaway played well, but his debut as point guard was

overshadowed by the Ewing-O'Neal matchup. Hardaway scored 13 points, had 5 assists, and 4 rebounds. More importantly, he played 36 of a possible 48 minutes. He had played well, but he knew he could do better, especially before national television cameras. His next opportunity to do just that came when he was selected to start for the first-ever NBA Schick Rookie All-Star game to be held in conjunction with the league's annual All-Star Weekend.

This year, the All-Star Weekend was to be held in Minneapolis, scene of both Hardaway's triumph in the 1990 Olympic Festival and failure against the University of Minnesota on New Year's Eve, 1992.

Minneapolis would once again be a proving ground for Hardaway. His basketball career development path seemed to be marked by appearances in that city—first as a skinny Prop 48 player, then as a young collegian, and now as an NBA rookie on the verge of stardom.

This time Minneapolis gave him the recognition he deserved. Reporters recognized him and lined up for interviews. The national spotlight was on him and on Coach K. C. Jones's rookie team, dubbed the Sensations.

Penny did not disappoint. He hit on 8 out of 9 shots from the field (including 2 three-pointers) in 22 minutes of play. Moreover, he played like a coach on the floor, directing the style of play and playing solid defense. After the game ended, he was presented with the first Schick rookie All-Star Game Most Valuable Player award. Things became easier for him after that.

The high point of Hardaway's great rookie year came that April at Boston Garden, when he matched his greatest college performances by registering a triple-double against the legendary Celtics. Penny scored 14 points, but, most significantly, he recorded 12 assists and pulled down 11 rebounds.

With one victory needed to cinch the first playoff appearance in the history of the Orlando Magic, the team entertained the Detroit Pistons before a packed house of 15,291 spectators at the Orlando Arena on April 8. The hometown fans could sense the electricity in the air as the Magic went through their pregame drills. The team, they noted, was displaying an intensity that was seldom seen in warm-ups. O'Neal, in particular, believed the night called for something special. He provided it not long after the opening tip-off. The Orlando center came through with a monster slam dunk. It shook the shot clock so violently that it stopped working for the rest of the game's first half.

Inspired, Hardaway and the rest of the Magic team played the rest of the game with great intensity. They quickly raced to a 58–39 lead. O'Neal was to wind up with 40 points and 15 rebounds, but his performance was nearly equaled by that of Hardaway, who had 26 points, 9 rebounds, and 9 assists. Seven of Hardaway's assists were recorded by halftime. Detroit's Joe Dumars's three-pointer, with 5 minutes left in the game, had pulled the Pistons within 9 points, but they got no closer. Hardaway and company outscored Detroit, 9–2, in the next 4 minutes, to push the margin to 115–99 with a minute to play. The final score was: Orlando 117, Detroit 103.

An indication of the magnitude of Orlando's success as a team was the fact that both the Magic and the Minnesota Timberwolves had entered the NBA as expansion teams in 1989. Typical of struggling expansion teams, Minnesota was on its way to a 20-win season in 1994. Orlando, on the other hand, would win 50 games.

At the season's close, league statisticians discovered that Hardaway was one of two rookies to start all 82 games (the Lakers' Nick Van Exel was the other). He averaged 15.9 points per game, fourth among NBA rookies. Further, he had

During his first season, Hardaway was one of only two rookies to start in all 82 games. Here, the Blazers just can't stop him as he heads up to the basket for 2 points.

6.6 assists per game and finished sixth in the entire NBA in steals with 2.3 per game.

As for his team, Orlando won a record 31 home games and 19 road contests. The subsequent NBA playoffs, however, were another story for the Magic. The team was quickly swept out of championship contention by the surprising Indiana Pacers in three games.

"We've got a great center (O'Neal)," Penny told reporters afterward, "and I'm going to work hard to develop all my talents at the point guard position. But we all have to come out and play hard every night. It's a team sport."

Anfernee Hardaway had learned that there is no "I" in the word *team*.

Chapter 6

The money controversy that surrounded Hardaway in 1993–94 did not let up as the 1993–94 season approached. His agents convinced him to demand a new contract with the Magic. His sparkling rookie season, they thought, was reason enough to seek one. Negotiations dragged, and Hardaway missed the first nine days of training camp before signing a $70 million, nine-year contract.

In his first exhibition game at the Orlando Arena, the fans booed him. "Sometimes the fans here make me feel wanted, and sometimes they don't," Hardaway shrugged.

The Orlando fans also expressed disappointment at the Magic's early exit from the 1994 playoffs. "We learned from the playoffs," Coach Hill told them. "We learned everything is different in the playoffs from the regular season. The defense is different. The officiating is different. Everything is different."

The Magic front office promised the fans a better showing in the new season. To back up their words, they obtained power forward Horace Grant, who had played flawlessly as a starter for the 1991, 1992, and 1993 NBA champion Chicago

Orlando won their opening home game against Philadelphia on November 5, 1994. Here, Hardaway aims to shoot as Sixers' defender Jeff Malone tries to block the shot.

Bulls. Horace Grant was a player with extensive successful playoff experience.

"I guarantee," Grant told the fans on his arrival, "that this season Orlando will not lose again in the first round of the NBA playoffs."

Nevertheless, the Magic's season began on a sour note on November 4, 1994. Orlando traveled to the U.S. Air Arena in Landover, Maryland, for the season opener against the Washington Bullets. The Bullets' Rex Chapman scored on a running jump shot, with one second showing on the clock, to give underdog Washington a 110–108 victory. Hardaway played 40 out of 48 possible minutes, but he scored only 14 points.

The taste of defeat didn't linger long. The following evening, the Magic opened their home season against the Philadelphia 76ers before a sellout crowd of 16,016 fans. Throughout the first half, Hardaway could hear a few scattered boos whenever he touched the ball, and, as the third quarter began, Philadelphia cut the Magic's lead to 64–54. Hardaway then silenced all critics when he led an Orlando fast break with a spectacular reverse layup to start a 10-point run for the Magic. Orlando went on to win, 122–107. Hardaway would see to it that the team would not lose at home until February 2.

Next, nearly twenty-four thousand people were on hand in Charlotte to watch the Magic take on the Hornets. Hardaway came through with 18 points, 8 assists, and 7 rebounds, but the headlines that night went to O'Neal, who scored 46 points in a 130–128 win. Madison Square Garden was the next stop as Orlando took on the New York Knicks, NBA championship finalists the season before. Hardaway starred with 27 points, but with 2 seconds remaining in the game, Knicks all-pro center Patrick Ewing scored on a 17-foot fadeaway shot to provide New York with a 101–99 win.

Their unimposing record of 2 wins and 2 losses was no indication of what would happen next for the Magic. Orlando traveled to Philadelphia and came away with an easy 116–103 win. The Magic would go on to win their next 8 games.

On November 21, at home against Miami, Hardaway scored 17 of his 30 points in the third quarter as the Magic broke open a close game. More significantly, this was accomplished with O'Neal sitting on the bench with 4 fouls. Prior to this, O'Neal's teammates had looked to him as their "go to" guy. On this night, Hardaway proved he, too, was capable of carrying his team and stepping up his game when O'Neal was absent. From that point, center O'Neal would have to share star billing with his point guard, Hardaway.

The Miami victory helped Hardaway's confidence to grow. Now no one criticized his position as team leader. Two nights later, against the defending world champion Houston Rockets, O'Neal once again found himself in third-quarter foul trouble and had to take a seat on the bench. The Rockets had cut the Orlando lead to 65–61, but Hardaway again rose to the occasion. He converted 4 free throws and a long three-point basket for a 72–63 Magic lead. Houston never challenged again, and they lost 117–94.

"Our success," Coach Hill said, "is as much a result of Penny Hardaway's play as anything else."

At Boston, Hardaway poured in 35 points in a 124–118 victory. He equaled that point total the following night against the Milwaukee Bucks. Around the league, the word was out: A new Magic Johnson had finally emerged. This one's home base was central Florida, not the Great Western Forum in Los Angeles. Hardaway, experts agreed, could score, rebound, play defense, and, more importantly, lead a team as well as Magic Johnson ever could.

The blossoming of Penny Hardaway coincided with the domination of the Orlando Magic over NBA foes. The team had been hitting on all cylinders. The Knicks arrived in Orlando on December 2 for a rematch of the November game Ewing had won for New York. This time, the game was no contest. Orlando scored its second consecutive victory over an NBA championship finalist when the Magic rocked the Knicks, 125–100. The deadly combination of Hardaway and O'Neal was so effective that, with one minute left to go in the third quarter, the pair had scored 64 points between them. The entire New York team was able only to manage 68 points. Afterward, sportswriters were buzzing with comparisons between the Hardaway and O'Neal combination and the legendary Los Angeles Lakers duo of Johnson and Jabbar.

The winning streak came to an end at Atlanta when Jon Koncak sank a tie-breaking free throw with 32 seconds remaining in the game and forced an Orlando turnover 25 seconds later. Each of the Magic's three losses had been by only 2 points. Three days later, Orlando went to Cleveland. The team took their frustrations out on the unsuspecting Cavaliers. They scored the game's first 8 points on vicious fast-break slam dunks by Hardaway and Donald Royal and 2 jumpers by Grant. Hardaway went on to score 10 points and O'Neal scored 9 in the Magic's 42-point first quarter. Orlando eventually won, 114–97. A quirk in the schedule resulted in the Magic facing Cleveland again the following night, this time at home at the Orlando Arena before another sellout crowd. In this game the Cavs slowed the tempo, waiting until the 24-second clock had run out before shooting. This tactic almost worked until Hardaway hit a three-pointer, and Orlando was off to a 10–0 run. The Magic won the low scoring game, 80–65.

Next was Miami. Hardaway scored 24 points and dished out 12 assists as Orlando breezed by 110–96. Atlanta was the next team to lose to the Magic. Red-hot Orlando was 15–3 with 13 wins in their last 14 games. A bump in the road came in New Jersey. Orlando made only 6 of 23 free throws and lost 128–101. The team then returned to home and winning ways, drubbing the Denver Nuggets, 120–106, after taking an 89–56 lead.

A West Coast road trip began with a win against Golden State, but Seattle handed the Magic their fifth defeat of the season, 124–84. As they had done previously, Orlando rebounded with a victory, 108–104, over Portland. In what was becoming a typical Hardaway performance, he scored 23 points and had 10 assists. Hardaway then pulled a hamstring in the Magic's win over the Los Angeles Clippers. As a result, he missed his first game as a professional two days later at home against Milwaukee.

The day after Christmas, the Magic were in Washington. The Bullets were overcome, 128–121. Hardaway's injury was completely forgotten as he played 47 minutes of the contest, scoring 29 with 11 assists. Orlando had won 21 games, losing only 5. Only Phoenix of the rival Western Conference at 20–6 had a comparable record.

A loss at Charlotte was sandwiched around wins over the

Miami Heat and the Los Angeles Clippers. Orlando celebrated the New Year with its fourteenth consecutive home victory, 113–110, over the Nets. Hardaway scored 33 points and led the Magic back from an 11-point deficit. Orlando led the Atlantic Division by seven games.

Guided by Hardaway and O'Neal, the Magic possessed the NBA's most potent offense. They averaged 113.6 points per game and had a remarkable 51.4 percent shooting average. Hardaway himself was averaging 22.5 points, 7 assists, 4 rebounds, and 7 steals per game.

After wins over Minnesota and Detroit, the team had won 24 out of its last 28 games, but were ambushed in Chicago by the Bulls. Led by All-Star forward Scottie Pippen, Chicago outscored Orlando, 30–13, in the third quarter and went on to a 109–77 win before 22,529 spectators. However, as in the past, the Magic took no time at all to regroup and beat the Pistons at home the following night, 124–107. Then, against the Atlanta Hawks, Hardaway hit 4 consecutive free throws in the final 15 seconds, to give Orlando a 101–96 win. Victories over Philadelphia, Charlotte, Dallas, and Denver followed.

Up next was Phoenix. The Suns had won 30 of 38 games and in the entire NBA ranked second only to the Magic. The game was nationally televised, and it lived up to fan expectations. It remained tied at the end of regulation play and went into overtime. What was not expected was a last-second duel between former Memphis Treadwell High School and Memphis State University teammates, and friends, Penny Hardaway and Elliot Perry.

With the game at stake, the Suns' Perry had possession of the ball and attempted to elude Hardaway. Perry fired a wild 18-foot shot that missed. The crowd noise was deafening as Phoenix and Orlando fought for the rebound. Most of the players failed to hear the referee's whistle, which had sounded

Hardaway operates one-on-one against J.R. Rider of the Minnesota
Timberwolves in one of many Orlando wins in the 1994–95 season.

as Perry released the ball. He had been fouled on his release
by his old friend Hardaway.

"I was surprised," Perry admitted later, "that they called a foul
on Penny in that situation. On the play before, I thought he got me
pretty good, and the officials didn't call anything." This time,
however, the whistle was blown, and Perry sank the winning free
throw for Phoenix in overtime. The final score was 111–110.

As they had in the past, the Magic players quickly
rebounded after a loss. This time the victim was Boston.
Orlando improved its record at the Orlando Arena to 19–0,
with a 110–97 win over the once mighty Celtics. The home
winning streak was to extend to 21 games before Seattle came
to town. Led by Gary Payton's 26 clutch points, Seattle
defeated the Magic, 106–103, before another sellout crowd.

National television appearances became commonplace for
Orlando, and the exposure added to Hardaway's fame. NBC

televised the Magic's 103–100 overtime win at home over the Knicks. In it, they highlighted Hardaway's pair of free throws that cemented the victory. After the final buzzer sounded, Orlando fans left their seats and mobbed Hardaway in a show of affection. "It took me a while," he told reporters with a smile, "but I'm finally happy to be in Orlando."

The 1995 NBA All-Star Weekend was another milepost in Hardaway's journey to superstardom. This time around, he did not play in the preliminary game as he had the year before in Minneapolis. He was elected starting point guard for the East squad and did not disappoint the voters. He played for 31 minutes in the annual All-Star Game, more than any other player. He also had 12 points, 11 assists, and 5 rebounds.

For Hardaway, the best was yet to come. The Magic improved their record to 41 wins against only 13 losses, with another win over Boston. This victory was different for Orlando, because after only five minutes had gone by into the game, O'Neal was ejected after shoving Celtic rookie center Eric Montross. Shaq had blown past Montross for 3 spectacular uncontested slamdunks when the altercation occurred. O'Neal was banished for the rest of the game and the subsequent match with the Chicago Bulls. After Shaq left, Hardaway and Nick Anderson each scored 27 points, and the Celtics quickly folded. Orlando won easily, 129–103.

The bright lights of NBC television were on Hardaway again on February 26, when the Bulls came to town. When it was over, his last-second slamdunk had given him a career-high 39 points. More importantly, it gave the Magic a 105–103 win.

"There is not a player in the league," reported Phil Taylor of *Sports Illustrated*, "whose future appears brighter than Penny Hardaway's."

As for Hardaway, all he wants is to see the Orlando Magic become the best team in the NBA.

Career Statistics

COLLEGE

Year	Team	GP	FG%	REB	PTS	AVG
1991–92	Memphis State	34	.433	237	590	17.4
1992–93	Memphis State	32	.477	273	729	22.8
Totals		66	.456	510	1319	20.0

NBA

Year	Team	GP	FG%	REB	AST	STL	BLK	PTS	AVG
1993–94	Orlando	82	.466	439	544	190	51	1313	16.0
1994–95	Orlando	77	.512	336	551	130	26	1613	20.9
Totals		159	.489	775	1095	320	77	2926	18.5

Where to Write Anfernee Hardaway

Mr. Anfernee Hardaway
c/o Orlando Magic
1 Magic Place
Orlando, FL 32801

Index

Pippen, Scottie, 10, 26, 59
Poston, Carl, 45-46, 47
Presley, Elvis, 21

R

Reeves, Khalid, 15
Reusse, Patrick, 35
Richardson, Nolan, 21, 30, 38
Riders, J.R., 18
Roberts, Selena, 49
Rodgers, Rodney, 15
Royal, Donald, 58
Ryan, Bob, 44

S

Scott, Dennis, 10
Skiles, Scott, 49, 50
Smith, Billy, 24, 28
Smith, Charles, 50
Stockton, John, 27

T

Taylor, Phil, 61
Tubbs, Nate, 34-35

V

Vaccaro, Sonny, 14, 23
Van Exel, Nick, 52
Vaughn, David, 28, 30, 39
Vitale, Dick, 38

W

Webber, Chris, 42, 43, 44, 46, 48
Wilfong, Win, 36
Williams, Brian, 47
Williams, Pat, 42, 43, 44, 47
Woodard, Alfre, 43
Wooden, John, 42

Z

Zinser, Lynn, 38